CANADA 2005

OUR PEOPLE. OUR EVENTS. OUR PERSPECTIVE.

Fans shield themselves from the rain during a synchronized swimming competition at the world aquatics championships in Montreal in July 2005. (Ryan Remiorz/CP)

CANADA 2005

OUR PEOPLE. OUR EVENTS. OUR PERSPECTIVE.

Editor: Patti Tasko
Photo Editor: Ron Poling

John Wiley & Sons Canada, Ltd.

Library and Archives Canada Cataloguing in Publication

Canadian Press

   Canada 2005: our people. our events. our perspective / The Canadian Press.

ISBN-13 978-0-470-83717-9
ISBN-10 0-470-83717-9

   1. Canada—History—21st century—Pictorial works.
2. Two thousand five, A.D.—Pictorial works.
I. Tasko, Patti II. Poling, Ron III. Title.

FC59.C3455 2005   971.07'1   C2005-904035-1

Production Credits:
Text editor: Patti Tasko, The Canadian Press
Photo editors: Ron Poling, Graeme Roy, The Canadian Press
Cover design: Ian Koo
Interior design: Adrian So
Front cover photo: Adrian Wyld, The Canadian Press
Back cover photos: Canadian Press Photos
Printer: Transcontinental

John Wiley & Sons Canada, Ltd.
6045 Freemont Blvd.,
Mississauga, Ontario
L5R 4J3

Printed in Canada
10 9 8 7 6 5 4 3 2 1

The Last Word. First.

Dear Reader,

This publication is a collection of our most prized images. Some of the images you may have seen before in your local newspaper. Others you may be seeing for the first time.

   High-quality prints of many of the photographs in this book may be purchased for personal use.

For information about acquiring CP images,

please visit us at http://www.cp.org/prints

or contact CP at 1-800-434-7578

or archives@cpimages.ca

CONTENTS

Yvonne Foster shares stories of her youth with family and friends the day before her 100th birthday at the General Continuing Care Centre in Edmonton in August 2005. (John Ulan/CP)

Former sergeant Roland Lafontaine of Papineauville, Que., places a flag on a friend's grave prior to a memorial ceremony in Ortona, Italy, in October 2004. (Ryan Remiorz/CP)

George Chuvalo, former Canadian heavyweight boxing champion, poses with his star after he is added to the Canadian Walk of Fame in Toronto in June 2005. (Tobin Grimshaw/CP)

Ray Betuzzi of Alberta competes in the men's 50-metre butterfly at the Canada Games in Regina in August 2005. (Jacques Boissinot/CP)

Margaret and Pierre Trudeau swing two-year-old son Sacha at the Vancouver Airport in October 1976. (Doug Ball/CP)

The coffin of Louis Sutter, patriarch of the Sutter hockey clan, is carried by his sons following his funeral in Viking, Alta., in February 2005. Left to right: Darryl, Brent, Ron, Brian, Duane and Rich.

Guillaume Dubois takes part in the annual Caribou Splash Cup in Mont Tremblant, Que., in April 2005 (Jonathan Hayward/CP)

INTRODUCTION

Sometimes it only takes a second to make a great picture. Other times it takes years.

Sometimes a news photographer has to be a bully, pushing through a crowd or onto a helicopter to get the shot. Other times, the photographer must be invisible.

Sometimes a good picture springs from serendipity – a beam of light falls just so. Other times, it takes planning – knowing when to bring along a ladder, for instance.

Sometimes, it just takes luck – although even then that luck must be perfectly executed.

In the pages of this book you will find all sorts of these photographs – from the big occasion that took days of planning to shoot, to the chance event that took place in a split second. It's an amazing record of a year in the life of our country, from the private to the public, the joyous to the tragic and all points in between.

Canadian Press journalists know they are privileged. They witness history in the making. "It's a great honour to get into people's lives and experience their trauma and convey it to Canadians," says photographer Adrian Wyld, who travelled with the Canadian military's disaster team in January when it provided relief to tsunami victims in Sri Lanka. "It's certainly worth the discomfort of travelling rough, eating military rations and sleeping on the ground," says Wyld.

The images of the past year have been particularly vivid. It was a year of tragedy – the death of a Canadian submariner from a fire on

Quebec politicians skate on the Place Youville rink in Quebec City in December 2004 in a stunt to encourage people to be more active. From the left, Education Minister Pierre Reid, Employment and Social Security Minister Claude Bechard, Health Minister Philippe Couillard, government mascot Vas-Y, Municipal Affairs Minister Jean-Marc Fournier and Family and Seniors Minister Carole Theberge. (Jacques Boissinot/CP)

the high seas, to the shooting of four young Mounties in Alberta. It was a year of drama—from the federal government that seemed about to fall several times, to the soap opera that was the Gomery inquiry. It was a year of marking significant events of yesterday—the 60th anniversary of the end of the Second World War and the 20th anniversary of the Air India bombing. It was a year that also had a lighter side—from the fun of the Calgary Stampede to the craziness of a massive rock concert. And of course there was the weather— everything from floods to tornadoes.

from a military vehicle parked in the middle of a Sri Lankan road to run his computer. "You go to a place like that, the last thing you're thinking is, I'm going to be able to use my cell," says Wyld. But that's how he filed pictures every night, until the vehicle's battery wore down or the cell signal disappeared – whichever came first.

Sometimes the challenge is logistical.

The British Royal Navy is towing a Canadian sub that caught fire at sea into a port somewhere in the United Kingdom. How do you get a photo of that?

down the detail that the sub would be arriving at Faslane naval base in Scotland. The military sent a helicopter but only the navy photographer and some TV crews were invited aboard. So Gunn, the lone Canadian news still photographer there, made various threats, including promising not to leave the base, until the Royal Navy found another helicopter to take him out. "You have to get that shot," he says, in explaining why he was so insistent. "It's a piece of Canadian history."

Sometimes, however, you have to be invisible.

Gunn covered the funeral for a mother and seven children, all killed in a house fire in the Niagara region of Ontario. In a situation like this, no photographer wants to intrude unnecessarily. "It was one of the most challenging things I've ever shot," Gunn says. "I had been out to the fire the first day and as the father of four kids, it was heartbreaking. When I took that shot a few days later, I was just bawling."

Sometimes the challenge is to stay alert.

Events such as the Gomery inquiry into the federal government's handling of sponsorship money in Quebec can drag on for months – and not offer a lot of exciting picture possibilities. "Three months of talking heads," recalls photographer Ryan Remiorz, who covered the Montreal leg of the inquiry. "Listening to lawyers and witnesses pour over thousands of pages of documents and invoices made concentrating both difficult and crucial. So little happens that when there is

"It's a great honour to get into people's lives and experience their trauma and convey it to Canadians."
– *Adrian Wyld,* CP photographer

CP's photographers are generally matter of fact about the challenge of shooting news photos, day after day, that tell stories in evocative ways.

Sometimes the challenge is technical.

Wyld was relying on a satellite telephone to file pictures from Sri Lanka back to Canada. Satellite phones can be a challenge for journalists because they don't use them every day – so just for the heck of it Wyld tried transmitting over his cellphone, using power

Photographer Frank Gunn concedes he had to resort to obnoxious behaviour. Gunn had flown to Britain to meet CP reporter Murray Brewster after news broke about a fire aboard HMCS *Chicoutimi*, a submarine Canada had purchased from Britain and was bringing home on its maiden Canadian voyage. One of the submariners had died of smoke inhalation. Gunn initially headed to Heathrow Airport, not sure where he would go after that. He managed to track some 'action' – someone gesturing, grimacing, crying or holding up a document – it's usually a fleeting moment so you have to try and keep your eye in the viewfinder constantly. This is harder than it sounds. The shooting position was also fixed so we couldn't move around much to try and come up with different angles."

Remiorz hits on another challenge – finding new ways to shoot the same old stuff.

Photographers alleviate the boredom of predictable pictures by looking for different ways to shoot the same old event. "Sports can be repetitive so you have to be creative," says Gunn. Maybe it's an oddball angle – zooming in on a tennis player while she is serving a ball so her face is in focus and the ball looks like it is lying on her cheek. Maybe it's catching an oddball expression. "There was this tennis player I just had to shoot because she did this funky thing with her cheeks," says Gunn. In the highly competitive world of sports photography, the horde of photographers lined up at the side of an event are always watching each other, says Gunn. Or they are listening to each other's cameras, trying to figure out, for instance, if someone is using an unusual shutter speed to produce a unique picture.

Gunn confesses that some photos that seem impressive are actually easy to shoot – the jockey caught in midair as he jumps off the horse the minute he wins the race (page 109). "You know he's known for that, so you just focus in on him and shoot." But sometimes

Prime Minister Paul Martin and his wife Sheila tour the Great Wall of China in January 2005. (Tom Hanson/CP)

everyone is focused on the same spot – the diving board at the Montreal aquatics championships, for example. And not everyone gets the shot of American diver Chelsea Davis hitting her face on the board as she descends (page 151). Remiorz did. "She began her dive and as I followed her up she smashed her head on the board with a thud that was heard around the pool and fell limp into the pool. When she came up there was a small trickle of blood on her forehead that soon turned into a torrent.... I kept shooting as they performed first aid and carried her away from the pool. It was only afterwards I checked my camera and saw that I had the moment of impact. Fortunately she wasn't injured too seriously. I wish I could say I timed it perfectly, but honestly the photo gods were smiling on me."

Gunn, who was also on the sidelines at the event and didn't get the shot, says Remiorz is being too humble. It's not just luck; "You have to execute it perfectly." For 10 years Gunn tried to capture a shot he knew existed of karate players doing their routine at sunrise on the Toronto waterfront. He tried different combinations to get the sun in just the right position. It finally came together one morning and the photo won a 2004 National Newspaper Award for feature photography (page 110).

Often it's the photographer's ability to deal with people that delivers the great shot, whether it is members of the Canadian Armed Forces on a stressful assignment or a family mourning the loss of a loved one. Wyld spent several years in the Canadian reserves so he could "talk the same language" as the DART team sent to Sri Lanka – and as a result they trusted him and shared news on photo opportunities with him. "The soldiers are co-operative because you are trying to convey back to Canada the reality of their assignment and what they are trying to accomplish." He also got to know them before the assignment started. "We travelled together for two days before I had to put a camera in their face." As for the Sri Lankans he met and photographed, they were even more welcoming. "They were very excited not to be forgotten."

Remiorz made similar connections when he went to the Netherlands in 2005 to cover the 60th anniversary of the end of the Second World War in Europe. "Travelling with these veterans and hearing their stories was fascinating.

"The highlight of the trip was the parade in Apeldoorn. There were wonderful moments to photograph everywhere I looked. The best one was of Sam Wormington. He was wearing a mint-condition uniform that he received two days before the war ended as he was being transferred. I had followed a group of veterans down this small road lined with people and was heading back to the main parade route when I saw Sam walking down the middle of the road by himself. As the crowd applauded louder he began raising his arms in celebration. It was just him and me walking down the street with a thousand Dutch cheering wildly. No TV, no dignitaries – just a beautiful moment." Judge for yourself: Remiorz's photo is on page 10.

Wyld also has a moment stuck in his mind from a busy year. On the front of this book is a photo he took at a memorial service on the Alexis reserve in Alberta for four RCMP constables slain during a stakeout in nearby Mayerthorpe. The service was held in a tiny church and photographers had to crowd in, the clicking of their cameras a constant reminder of their presence. "It was very intrusive," says Wyld, "but they were so accommodating." At the end of the service, drums were brought in and an aboriginal song that symbolized the spirit of the RCMP officers being sent to the sky was performed. "It was one of the few times I've seen when no photographers took any pictures," says Wyld. "They just wanted to be respectful."

That's one picture we can't share with you. But there are hundreds of others we hope you will find just as moving.

Enjoy.

Patti Tasko

Toronto Blue Jays players cast long shadows at spring training in Dunedin, Florida in February 2005. (Frank Gunn/CP)

SALUTING MEMORIES: Remembering the Second World War

The Italian campaign

Bill (Skull) Worton stood on the beach in Pachino, Sicily, where he landed with other Canadian troops on July 10, 1943. He gazed up the shoreline to the spot where his war began with sudden brutal consequences.

The 22-year-old private with the Seaforth Highlanders was part of an armada of 183,000 allied troops launching the invasion of Italy. The door opened and Worton turned to see the British coxswain who was operating their landing craft take a bullet in the head. "The poor kid never knew what hit him," said Worton, of Edith, Alta. "I don't think it was anything but our own fire crossing that thing."

When a pilgrimage of Canadian veterans of the 22-month long campaign, including Worton, returned to the area on Sicily's southern shore in October 2004, they dipped their hands and feet in the Mediterranean where most entered their baptism of fire. They gazed over the hills they humped, and they walked through the Canadian war cemetery at Agira. "This was where the war hit me because I knew these men well," said Worton. "We were like brothers."

About 93,000 Canadians served in Italy. Nearly 6,000 were killed.

– Stephen Thorne, CP

Gov. Gen. Adrienne Clarkson lays a wreath at the monument overlooking the battlegrounds of Casa Bernardi in Ortona to mark the 60th anniversary of the end of the Italian campaign of the Second World War. (Ryan Remiorz/CP)

Ernest (Smokey) Smith, who received a Victoria Cross for his actions during the Italian campaign, gets a kiss from a schoolgirl following a memorial service at the Moro River Cemetery in Ortona. (Ryan Remiorz/CP)

Former sergeant Harvey Brush of Wiarton, Ont., offers a tribute to the fallen at the battlegrounds of Casa Bernardi. (Ryan Remiorz/CP)

Former sergeant Walter Barnum of Parksville, B.C., walks among the Canadian graves at the Commonwealth cemetery in Cassino, Italy, on Oct. 26, 2004. (Ryan Remiorz/CP)

Liberation of the Netherlands

It's a debt they insist can never be repaid, but thousands of grateful Dutch residents offered their Canadian liberators flowers, oranges, beer and kisses during the 60th anniversary celebrations of the Liberation of the Netherlands in May 2005.

Hundreds of thousands of people – families representing three generations and some who drove for hours – attended parades and services honouring 1,500 Canadian war veterans who came back for the anniversary, expected to be the last one on such a scale. Young children rushed to slap hands with the veterans with a fervour normally reserved for pop stars and sports heroes.

Canadians played a major role in liberating the Netherlands from occupation by Hitler's Nazi Germany, with 7,600 Canadian soldiers dying in the country. And the Dutch have always shown their gratitude on the anniversary. Jessica Stender, a young mother who brought her two children in a stroller to a parade in Apeldoorn, handed out 100 yellow tulips to the soldiers. "Every time there's a war somewhere, I realize that we live here in peace," said Stender.

– Michelle MacAfee, CP

A Canadian veteran and his caregiver salute as they pass Prince William Alexander, left, during a parade to mark the 60th anniversary of the liberation of the Netherlands in Wageningen. (Ryan Remiorz/CP)

Canadian veteran Sam Wormington of Kamloops, B.C., celebrates during the veterans' parade marking the 60th anniversary of VE-Day in Apeldoorn, Netherlands. (Ryan Remiorz/CP)

A Canadian veteran reaches out to shake a child's hand during the veterans' parade in Apeldoorn. (Ryan Remiorz/CP)

Canadian veterans Ernest (Smokey) Smith, left, and Howard Anderson, a former Cree chief from the Gordon First Nation in Saskatchewan, share a laugh at the Apeldoorn ceremonies. (Ryan Remiorz/CP)

Smith shows his medals, including the Victoria Cross, the Commonwealth's highest military honour, at a ceremony for him in Cesena, Italy, in October 2004. Smith died in 2005. (Ryan Remiorz/CP)

Canadian veteran Frank Graham of Midland, Ont., gets a hug from a Dutch woman in Apeldoorn. (Ryan Remiorz/CP)

TORN FROM THE PAGES: A year of headlines

HMCS *Chicoutimi* makes its way into Faslane naval base in Scotland on Oct. 10, 2004. (Frank Gunn/CP)

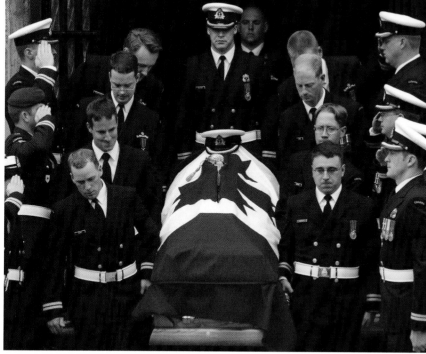

Fire hits submarine on maiden Canadian voyage

Cmdr. Luc Pelletier described it as "probably one of the worst nightmares you can have as a submariner." The Canadian Forces had just taken control of HMCS *Chicoutimi*, one of four subs purchased from Britain, and it was only a few days out of port when it was hit with a fire on Oct. 5, 2004, turning it into a deadly, smoke-filled chimney. Several crew members suffered smoke inhalation before the fire could be controlled and were airlifted to hospital while the sub was towed to Scotland. Lieut. Chris Saunders, 32, a Halifax father of two, who had transferred to Chicoutimi only two weeks earlier, died in hospital. It was later determined the fire started when high-voltage cables short-circuited after being immersed in sea water.

The coffin of Lieut. Chris Saunders is carried from St. Andrew's Church in Halifax. (Andrew Vaughan/CP)

The flag flies at half-mast as the crew of HMCS *Chicoutimi* stand in their conning tower on the way into Faslane naval base. Damaged tiles are visible on the tower. (Frank Gunn/CP)

Gov. Gen. Adrienne Clarkson dresses down for the annual press gallery dinner in Ottawa in October 2004. Clarkson was playing off criticism her office spent too much money. (Jonathan Hayward/CP)

Steven Truscott, right, convicted at the age of 14 of murder, stands with his son Ryan and wife Marlene outside their home in Guelph, Ont., in October 2004. Truscott had just learned that federal Justice Minister Irwin Cotler was not going to overturn his conviction, even though there was a "reasonable basis" to conclude it was a miscarriage of justice. (Adrian Wyld/CP)

Ellen Fairclough

Canada's first female cabinet minister was often called a trailblazer for women. Appointed secretary of state in 1957, the native of Hamilton was also Canada's first female postmaster general and the first woman to serve as acting prime minister. Fairclough was an outspoken advocate for women's rights, fighting for private members' bills on equal pay for equal work and banning discrimination in hiring on the basis of sex, race and religion.

Marc Woerlen, 41, carries the coffin of his 19-month-old daughter Debora following a memorial service in November 2004. Woerlen's pregnant wife and seven children – ranging in age from 19 months to 11 years – died in a farmhouse fire in the southern Ontario community of West Lincoln. Woerlen, who was in Ottawa at the time of the fire, heard the horrifying news from his father over the phone. (Frank Gunn/CP)

Gomery inquiry: The best show in town

Former public works minister Alfonso Gagliano sits behind a pillar, waiting to testify at the Gomery inquiry in Ottawa in February. (Jonathan Hayward/CP)

The head of the sponsorship scandal inquiry, Justice John Gomery, addresses the hearings in April. (Paul Chiasson/CP)

For some people, the Gomery inquiry into what happened to millions of public dollars spent by the government on a sponsorship program was more entertaining than anything on TV. Even Quebec Superior Court Justice John Gomery, who headed the inquiry, said he had the best seat in town.

Public testimony began in September 2004, and it wasn't long before allegations of government money being redirected into ad agencies with Liberal ties came out. Former prime minister Jean Chrétien told the inquiry the program was part of a strategy to increase Canada's profile in Quebec. He also used his appearance to show off some personalized golf balls he had received from world leaders, in a swipe at Gomery who had criticized such souvenirs for being small-town.

Ad executive Paul Coffin testified he had repeatedly produced fake invoices and overbilled the federal government for work that was never done, at the request of bureaucrat Chuck Guité. Guité, who had first maintained there was no political interference in awarding contracts, contradicted that in later testimony, saying it was completely politically driven.

Public testimony ended in June, about the same time Paul Martin's Liberals managed to squeak their way through the spring session of Parliament without losing the government.

Former prime minister Jean Chrétien displays a golf ball during his testimony at the inquiry in Ottawa in February. (Jonathan Hayward/CP)

Roger Thomas organizes a 180,000-page complete set of Gomery transcripts and evidence in Montreal in June. Thomas worked 14-hour days overseeing the copying and distribution of the transcripts and his office produced more than eight million photocopies. (Ian Barrett/CP)

Former public works minister Alfonso Gagliano walks down a corridor after giving his final testimony in Ottawa in February. (Fred Chartrand/CP)

Some of the faces at the Gomery inquiry, from left to right, top to bottom: Chuck Guité, Paul Martin, Diane Deslauriers, Alfonso Gagliano, Jean Pelletier, Giuseppe Morselli, Jacques Corriveau, Jean Brault, Michel Beliveau, Daniel Dezainde, Bernard Thiboutot and Claude Boulay (Fred Chartrand, Paul Chiasson, Tom Hanson, Jonathan Hayward, Ryan Remiorz, Francois Roy/CP)

Alfonso Gagliano takes a stroll during a break in his second day of testimony at the sponsorship inquiry. (Fred Chartrand/CP)

Ad man Paul Coffin, the first person charged in the federal sponsorship scandal, leaves the courthouse in Montreal in May after pleading guilty to 15 fraud charges. (Ryan Remiorz/CP)

Justice John Gomery leaves the inquiry in Ottawa in January. (Jonathan Hayward/CP)

U.S. President George W. Bush and Prime Minister Paul Martin pose together in November 2004 after Bush arrives at Parliament Hill for his first official visit to Canada. (Tom Hanson/CP)

1920 - 2004

Arthur Hailey

Hailey was a bestselling author who plucked characters from ordinary life and threw them into extraordinary ordeals. British-born, Hailey began his writing career in Canada and later retired to the Bahamas. Millions of copies of his 11 books, which included *The Final Diagnosis*, *Airport* and *Hotel*, were published in 40 countries and 38 languages. Several were made into movies, including *Airport*, which inspired a series of disaster movies in the 1970s and later parodies such as *Airplane!*

A child's note to veterans is placed on the Tomb of the Unknown Soldier following Remembrance Day ceremonies in Ottawa on Nov. 11, 2004. (Tom Hanson/CP)

The Snowbirds, the Canadian Forces acrobatic team, do a fly-by in the missing man formation at a memorial service for Capt. Miles Selby, who died in a fiery collision during a training session in Moose Jaw, Sask., in December 2004. (Troy Fleece/CP)

Investigators search a field for debris after the crash of the Snowbird jet that killed Capt. Miles Selby. (Troy Fleece/CP)

Mammoth tsunami in Indian Ocean reverberates around the world

Canada sent 200 soldiers, part of the military's Disaster Assistance Response Team, into Sri Lanka to help cope with the devastating aftermath of the tsunami that hit parts of southern Asia around the Indian Ocean in December 2004.

From a base in Ampara, the DART team offered clean water, medical aid and reconstruction help to survivors. They were inundated with stories of horrific loss. The medics treated a teenage girl who hadn't spoken since her whole family was washed away. There were haunted adults who stared off into space, not speaking and refusing to eat.

Other Canadians helped out too. Consular staff in Phuket, Thailand, walked through a huge morgue countless times trying to help Canadian families find their loved ones. Expatriates voluntarily spent harrowing days searching for Canadians and recovering bodies.

More than 200,000 people were killed or missing in 11 countries after the tsunami.

A mother watches as Capt. Carmen Meakin of the Canadian Forces examines a young boy at a temporary medical clinic in Kalmunai, Sri Lanka, in January 2005. (Adrian Wyld/CP)

Gunner Clayton Comeau, from Miramichi, N.B., helps a woman out of an assault boat shuttling residents across a bay in Pottuvil, Sri Lanka, in January. (Adrian Wyld/CP)

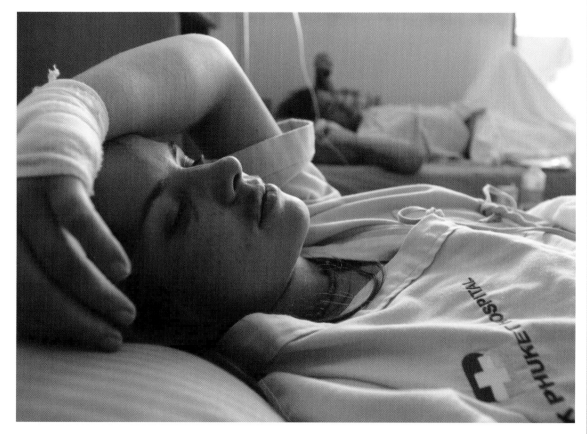

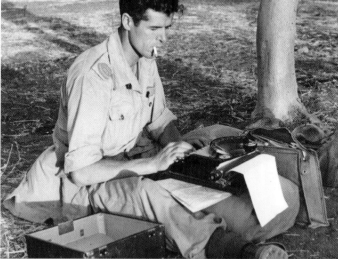

The long-time Canadian Press journalist was an unflappable war correspondent who landed with Canadian invasion troops in Italy and France, then described the Allied defeat and subsequent Japanese surrender at Hong Kong that ended the Second World War. His copy was written in the classic wire-service style of the day – spare, crisp, but meticulous in its detail with flashes of brilliant colour.

Canadian tsunami survivor Rachel Gobeil, 27, of Les Escoumeins, Que., recovers at Bangkok Phuket Hospital. Gobeil suffered hip and spinal injuries when she was hit by a wave on the island of Koh Phi Phi, south of Phuket. (Deddeda Stemler/CP)

Master Cpl. John Nicholson, from Dominion N.S., films damage in Kalmunai, Sri Lanka, in January. (Adrian Wyld/CP)

Rescue and clean-up crew survey a flooded lobby at the Seapearl Beach Hotel along Patong Beach on Phuket Island, Thailand, in December 2004. (Deddeda Stemler/CP)

A cyclist travels the frost-covered seawall in Vancouver's Stanley Park in January. (Chuck Stoody/CP)

Skiers carrying red glow sticks make their way down the mountain during an annual New Year's Eve ski at Silver Star ski resort in Vernon, B.C. (Jeff Bassett/CP)

Canada geese fly above the South Saskatchewan River, which was steaming in -18 C weather in Medicine Hat, Alta., on New Year's Day 2005. (J.P. Moczulski/CP)

Prime Minister Paul Martin visits the Forbidden City in Beijing during a January trip to promote Canada-China trade. (Tom Hanson/CP)

A reporter looks over the remains of two homes destroyed in a mudslide in North Vancouver in January. (Chuck Stoody/CP)

A great grey owl dives after prey beneath the snow in a field near Ottawa in January. The owls had moved into eastern Ontario in abundance because of a shortage of prey in their usual hunting grounds farther north. (Jonathan Hayward/CP)

1933 - 2005

Lois Hole

Hole was Alberta's much-loved 15th lieutenant-governor when she died, but she was better known across the country as a gardening expert, dispensing advice to green thumbs across the country from her family's nursery business in St. Albert. Hole was also known as the Queen of Hugs – whether she was conferring a university degree, meeting a young girl guide or advising a fellow garden enthusiast, she hugged them all. "Even the flowers are crying," said Sharon Mavko, a gardening customer, after her death.

Two bald eagles perch on a channel buoy to Vancouver's Granville Island in January. (Chuck Stoody/CP)

In a rare sight in Toronto's financial district, an RCMP officer pulls cases into the offices of Scotiabank after a search warrant was executed in the investigation into Royal Group Technologies Inc. for alleged price-fixing and improper accounting. (Frank Gunn/CP)

Staff Gen. Ray Henault (left), the outgoing chief of national defence, and Gen. Rick Hillier, the incoming chief, stand together during a change of command ceremony in Ottawa in February 2005. (Fred Chartrand/CP)

John Matheson attends a ceremony in Kingston, Ont., marking the 40th anniversary of the Canadian flag. As a Liberal MP, Matheson helped then-prime minister Lester Pearson stickhandle the flag bill through an acrimonious debate in the House of Commons in the mid-1960s. (Tom Hanson/CP)

39

Team Chateau Frontenac, skipped by Michel Lessard, races to the finish line to win an ice canoe race on the St. Lawrence River at the Quebec Winter Carnival in February. (Jacques Boissinot/CP)

Kids from Ottawa's West-End Wolverines play shinny hockey on the Rideau Canal in Ottawa in February, as part of Hockey Day in Canada. The event was held a few days after the NHL officially cancelled its 2004–2005 season. (Tom Hanson/CP)

RCMP stakeout turns into tragedy

The storage hut on the Roszko farm near Mayerthorpe, Alta., where four Mounties were shot and killed. (Jeff McIntosh/CP)

Assistant RCMP Commissioner Bill Sweeney could barely find words that March afternoon in the usually peaceful farming community of Mayerthorpe, Alta. Four Mounties—"brave, young officers," Sweeney called them—had been gunned down in an almost incomprehensible series of events.

It began as a stakeout over stolen vehicles and a marijuana grow-op. But it went catastrophically wrong when James Roszko walked into his Quonset hut to confront constables Peter Schiemann, Leo Johnston, Brock Myrol and Anthony Gordon. Armed with three guns, Roszko cut them down and then turned one of his weapons on himself.

Canada soon learned who the 47-year-old Roszko was: a cop-hating loner, a convicted sexual predator, a man who had kept his community fearful for 15 years. His own father called him a "devil."

And Canada soon learned what it had lost: The oldest of the dead officers was 32; the youngest, 25. One was fresh out of RCMP training school. All were mourned as officers and friends, men who coached minor hockey, raised money for cancer patients and spoke at nearby reserves. It reminded an increasingly big-city country how important the national police force remains to its small-town roots.

At a national memorial in Edmonton, a kilometre-long parade of law enforcement officers from across North America marched in their honour, led by hundreds of red-serge-clad Mounties, the tramp of their boots beating time to the skirl of bagpipes.

Questions arose. Some said police should have known Roszko was a threat; others maintained police can't predict when a suspect becomes a predator. An investigation was struck.

What remains is awe and sorrow at their sacrifice, said Gov. Gen. Adrienne Clarkson at the memorial. "These men so cared about the public good that they were willing to die to serve it."

– Bob Weber, CP

RCMP members lower the flag and mourners leave flowers at the Mayerthorpe RCMP detachment. (Jeff McIntosh/CP)

Alberta Premier Ralph Klein, left, and RCMP Commissioner Giuliano Zaccardelli attend a memorial service for the slain RCMP constables. (Jeff McIntosh/CP)

RCMP headdress-bearers, followed by officers, march to the memorial in Edmonton for the four officers killed in the stakeout. (Adrian Wyld/CP)

Cpl. Joan Kuyp, Const. Joe Sangster, Const. Bethany Hoskin, and Const. Jason Lapointe (left to right) attend the memorial service. The four carried the headdresses of their slain colleagues. (Larry MacDougal/CP)

An RCMP officer salutes the hearse carrying the body of Const. Brock Myrol following his funeral in Red Deer, Alta. (Jeff McIntosh/CP)

RCMP Const. Lee Johnston helps carry the coffin of his twin brother, Const. Leo Johnston, following his funeral in Lac La Biche, Alta. (Tom Hanson/CP)

Const. Leo Johnston's wife Kelly at her husband's funeral in Lac La Biche. (Tom Hanson/CP)

Retired Canadian Forces general Romeo Dallaire is applauded in March at Government House in Ottawa after he was presented with the Pearson Peace Medal. Dallaire led a United Nations peacekeeping mission in Rwanda in 1994 and he wrote an award-winning book on the genocide he witnessed in the region. (Fred Chartrand/CP)

Michel Leblanc, founder of the discount airline Jetsgo, talks to a reporter in his Montreal office. Jetsgo went bankrupt in March 2005, leaving passengers stranded before spring break. (Ryan Remiorz/CP)

Jetsgo planes sit idle on the tarmac of Quebec City's Jean-Lesage Airport. (Jacques Boissinot/CP)

A seal hunter walks along a bloody path on an ice floe in the Gulf of St. Lawrence in April. The annual hunt always causes conflict between hunters, who say it is a necessary part of the region's economy and helps keep the seal population under control, and their opponents, who maintain there's no scientific basis for killing thousands of the mammals each year. (Jonathan Hayward/CP)

Death of a Pope

Cardinals bless the remains of Pope John Paul II during his funeral mass in St. Peter's Square in Rome on April 8. The mass drew millions to the Vatican, including presidents, prime ministers and kings. (Tom Hanson/CP)

Mourners, one with a Canadian flag, pray during John Paul's funeral mass. (Tom Hanson/CP)

Civil servants from 18 federal government departments work in the master control cell during an anti-terrorism drill in Gatineau, Que., in April. (Jonathan Hayward/CP)

Saul Bellow

The Nobel Prize-winning author of *Herzog* and *Humboldt's Gift* was a master of comic melancholy. Born in Lachine, Que., he moved to Chicago as a child. He became the most acclaimed of a generation of Jewish writers who emerged after the Second World War. "The backbone of 20th-century American literature has been provided by two novelists – William Faulkner and Saul Bellow," fellow writer Philip Roth said after his death.

Conservative Leader Stephen Harper speaks to thousands of people opposed to same-sex marriage who marched on Parliament Hill in April 2005. Three months later, Canada became the fourth country in the world to sanction same-sex marriage. (Jonathan Hayward/CP)

Liberals face nail-biting year

It was all about staying in power. Paul Martin's minority Liberal government managed to hang on in its first year through a combination of methods so nefarious – and successful – that the opposition Conservatives compared them to crooks, Satan and Hollywood homicidal maniac Hannibal Lecter.

Thrown about by allegations of government kickbacks and dirty politics that came out almost daily from Quebec Justice John Gomery's sponsorship inquiry, the Liberals were vulnerable. Martin was desperate enough to beg the nation in a TV address to give him more time to deal with the sponsorship scandal. Then he was held hostage over the spring budget by the NDP, who insisted he erase corporate tax cuts and replace them with spending on housing, the environment, education and foreign aid. Because the Liberals needed NDP support to pass the budget, they agreed, which incensed the Conservatives, who tried to topple them at every turn. No Liberal, not even the sickest MP, dared to leave Ottawa for fear the government would fall on one vote.

Martin's most dramatic move – using a cabinet job to entice star Tory MP Belinda Stronach to join the government side – provided short-term pain relief. But the advantage was lost when some of his own MPs left because they couldn't support the government's same-sex marriage legislation. Around the same time came allegations from a Conservative MP that the Liberals were trying to buy his vote.

The spring session of Parliament finally ended in late June with a little-used procedural tactic that bamboozled furious Conservatives and managed to get the contentious Liberal-NDP budget amendments through the Commons. The politicians went off for the summer, and only political junkies missed the daily hijinks.

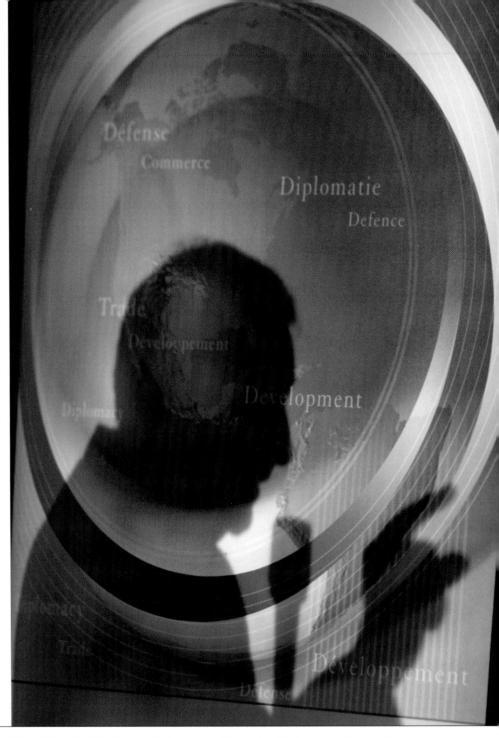

Prime Minister Paul Martin casts a shadow on a backdrop as he talks about a new foreign policy paper in Gatineau, Que., in April. (Tom Hanson/CP)

In a TV appearance from his office on Parliament Hill on April 21, Prime Minister Martin asks Canadians to give his government more time to deal with the sponsorship scandal. (Tom Hanson/CP)

Prime Minister Paul Martin smiles alongside Belinda Stronach in May after they announce Stronach is leaving the Conservatives to join the Liberals as human resources minister. (Tom Hanson/CP)

Martin speaks on Canada's new foreign policy paper in Gatineau, Que., in April. (Tom Hanson/CP)

Conservative Party Leader Stephen Harper plays football with deputy leader Peter MacKay on Parliament Hill in June. (Jake Wright/CP)

Conservative Leader Stephen Harper whispers to Bloc Québécois Leader Gilles Duceppe during a Holocaust remembrance ceremony on Parliament Hill in May. (Tom Hanson/CP)

The Queen, sitting next to Chief Alphonse Bird, visited the First Nations University in Regina during her nine-day visit to Saskatchewan and Alberta to mark the centennials of the provinces' entry into Confederation. (Paul Chiasson/CP)

The Queen pets some corgis after visiting the Alberta legislature. (Paul Chiasson/CP)

Justin Trudeau, son of former prime minister Pierre Trudeau, kisses his new bride Sophie Gregoire after their wedding in Montreal in May. (Ryan Remiorz/CP)

A tornado touches down in a field west of Lethbridge, Alta., in June. Although a fierce hail storm followed, no damage from the funnel cloud was reported. (David Rossiter/ *Lethbridge Herald*)

Tim Cook rides a homemade skim board as his friend Tyson McEachern waits his turn on Fancy Lake in Conquerall Mills, N.S. Heavy rains raised the water levels in area lakes in May, causing flooding and forcing some evacuations. (Andrew Vaughan/CP)

Bill Rogers of High River, Alta., picks up debris from the fifth fairway of the Highwood Golf Club, which passes by his house, in June 2005. Heavy rains flooded a section of the town. (Jeff McIntosh/CP)

Art Jervis wades through his flooded yard in front of his home along the Red Deer River in Drumheller, Alta., in June. (Jason Scott/CP)

A technician works on lines near a toppled transmission tower in Dartmouth in November 2004 after a winter storm hit Nova Scotia, leaving 100,000 homes and businesses without power. (Andrew Vaughan/CP)

1948 - 2005

Chuck Cadman

Once mistaken for a janitor in his own parliamentary office, the ponytailed Independent MP played a key role in the Commons on May 19, 2005. Cadman, dressed in jeans and chewing gum, calmly stood up and cast his vote for the Liberal minority government in a confidence motion, sparing Canadians a summer election. He had shown up in Ottawa shortly after completing chemotherapy for skin cancer, saying he was there on behalf of constituents opposed to another election.

The summer of 2005 was long and hot in Ontario. Clouds float by as a lifeguard keeps watch over a river beach in Ottawa in August. (Jonathan Hayward/CP)

Jan Luedecke rides a wave in Lake Ontario as the remnants of hurricane Katrina pass through Toronto in August 2005. (Adrian Wyld/CP)

"It was an unimaginable loss. It was your loss. It was our nation's loss."
– *Prime Minister Paul Martin.*

Amid the sound of waves pounding the shore, families, friends and politicians from Ireland, India and Canada paid tribute June 23, 2005 to the 329 victims of the Air India bombing 20 years earlier off the coast of Ireland.

The 500 mourners held a minute of silence at 8:12 a.m.; Air India Flight 182 disappeared from the radar at 8:13 a.m. on June 23, 1985, blown apart by a bomb planted in Canada. It was a particularly tough anniversary for families of victims: two months earlier, two B.C. men charged in the bombing had been acquitted.

Prime Minister Paul Martin, Irish President Mary McAleese (second right) and family members of those killed in the crash carry candles to the sea at Ahakista, Ireland. (Fred Chartrand/CP)

Relatives and friends of victims of the Air India crash place candles in the sea. (Fred Chartrand/CP)

PQ leader calls it quits

Parti Québécois Leader Bernard Landry shocked his party and his province on June 4, 2005, when he resigned after the results of a vote on his leadership were announced. Landry, who took over as premier from Lucien Bouchard in 2001 but lost the 2003 election to Liberal Jean Charest, had said he would stay on if he achieved a score of at least 76 per cent and his mark, only slightly above that threshold, wasn't good enough for him. Landry was first elected in 1976 with the first Parti Québécois government under René Lévesque. "To assume a position like mine, the one of René Lévesque and his successors, you have to have a support that is solid, indisputable, massive," Landry said, choking as he said Lévesque's name.

His wife, Chantal Renaud, looks on as Bernard Landry announces he is resigning the leadership of the Parti Québécois. (Clement Allard/CP)

Quebecers celebrate Fête Nationale on the Plains of Abraham in Quebec City in June. (Jacques Boissinot/CP)

A giant flag makes an appearance at the Canada Day parade on Ste-Catherine Street in Montreal. (David Boily/CP)

Happy birthday, Canada

Prime Minister Paul Martin holds up the original Maple Leaf flag that fluttered atop the Peace Tower in 1965, during Canada Day celebrations on Parliament Hill in Ottawa. (Tom Hanson/CP)

The Canadian Air Force's Snowbirds fly in formation over the Peace Tower for Canada Day celebrations. (Tom Hanson/CP)

A salesman watches an interview with Karla Homolka on television station RDI in Montreal in July. Homolka, the notorious ex-wife of convicted killer Paul Bernardo, had just left the Ste-Anne-des-Plaines prison north of Montreal after serving her 12-year sentence for manslaughter in the sex slayings of two Ontario teenagers. (Ryan Remiorz/CP)

A red van believed to be carrying Karla Homolka leaves the prison in Ste-Anne-des-Plaines, Que. (Paul Chiasson/CP)

Hardware store owner Richer Lapointe, who hired killer Karla Homolka after she got out of prison in June 2005, holds the tape recorder he used to tape their conversations, which he gave to a newspaper. (Ryan Remiorz/CP)

A freight train rolls past work crews removing tanker cars from the tracks in Prescott, Ont., in July after a train derailed. The tanks were empty and there were no injuries in the crash. (Jonathan Hayward/CP)

Police officers patrol the Montreal subway in July as security is beefed up after suicide bombers attacked the London transit system, killing 56 people during morning rush hour. (Paul Chiasson/CP)

Thrill seekers enjoy a roller-coaster ride at the Calgary Stampede in July. (Jeff McIntosh/CP)

Members of the Canadian Auto Workers union (left) shake hands with members of Ford Motor Co. of Canada in July, before the second day of meetings to settle new contracts with the Big Three auto producers. (Tobin Grimshaw/CP)

Handlers herd cattle into the ring at the auction market in Strathmore, Alta., in July. Hours earlier, the United States had opened the border to Canadian cattle, closed since May 2003 following the discovery of a case of mad cow disease in Alberta. (Larry MacDougal/CP)

Douglas Lapierre of Chezzetcook, N.S., looks at a new monument on the Halifax waterfront that honours the memory of the 10,000 French-speaking Acadians who were forced out of the Maritimes by England 250 years ago. (Andrew Vaughan/CP)

John Dockman of Airdrie, Alta., tries to avoid a bull during the running of the bulls in Strathmore, Alta., in July. (Jeff McIntosh/CP)

Wrapped in blankets, passengers from an Air France plane are directed into a holding room at Pearson Airport in Toronto. More than 300 people escaped with their lives after the jet skidded off the runway and then burst into flames during a fierce thunderstorm. (Frank Gunn/CP)

A man watches from nearby Highway 401 as the tail section of the Air France passenger jet burns. (Jorge Rios/CP)

A fire truck hoses down the wreckage of Air France flight 358. (Frank Gunn/CP)

Gov. Gen. Adrienne Clarkson and Gen. Rick Hillier, newly named as chief of national defence staff, review the guard during a change of command ceremony in Ottawa in February 2005. (Fred Chartrand/CP)

Ernest (Smokey) Smith

Arguably Canada's best-known veteran, Smith was the last winner of the Victoria Cross for bravery beyond the call of duty and the only Canadian private to win the medal, the Commonwealth's highest decoration for heroism. A joyful man with an impish smile, he single-handedly fought off German tanks and troops in 1944 during the crossing of the Savio River in northern Italy in the push to break the Germans' Gothic Line.

Michaelle Jean, just named Canada's next Governor General, stands with her husband Jean-Daniel Lafond and her daughter Marie-Eden, six, at an Ottawa news conference in August 2005. (Fred Chartrand/CP)

An advance party of 25 Red Cross volunteers board a Canadian Forces aircraft in Trenton, Ont., in September 2005. They are headed to the southern United States to help with disaster relief after Hurricane Katrina devastated the region. (Frank O'Connor/CP)

Dan Cooper rides his bike in Ottawa past an ad for a bike store that uses high gasoline prices as a marketing technique in August 2005. (Jonathan Hayward/CP)

Dani Estabhan changes the price of a litre of regular gasoline at a station in Montreal in August 2005. Gas prices spiked sharply in the late summer because of rising crude prices and the effects of Hurricane Katrina, which disrupted refining operations in the Gulf of Mexico. (Ryan Remiorz/CP)

Prime Minister Paul Martin, left, gets some dancing pointers from Adrian Lachance at the Flying Dust First Nations annual pow wow in Meadow Lake, Sask., in September 2005. (Jeff McIntosh/CP)

Picketing CBC employees are reflected in a window bearing the broadcaster's logo in Ottawa in August 2005. The CBC locked out 5,500 employees after the broadcaster and the Canadian Media Guild could not agree on a contract. (Jonathan Hayward/CP)

Fireworks explode over the legislature building in Edmonton as part of Alberta's centennial celebrations in September 2005. (Darryl Dyck/*Edmonton Sun*)

Hat tricks

Defence Minister Bill Graham adjusts his helmet as he prepares for a tour of CFB Gagetown, N.B., in an armoured vehicle in January. (Andrew Vaughan/CP)

Prime Minister Paul Martin wears a hat presented to him during a ceremony opening a school in Tanghin, Burkina Faso during a November 2004 trip. (Adrian Wyld/CP)

"Distrust any enterprise
that requires new clothes."
– H.D. Thoreau (1817-1862)

Conservative leader Stephen Harper, left, waves to the crowd as he participates in the Calgary Stampede parade in July. (Jeff McIntosh/CP)

Gov. Gen. Adrienne Clarkson and Prime Minister Paul Martin are both protected from the sun during Canada Day celebrations on Parliament Hill. (Tom Hanson/CP)

ENTERTAINING CANADIANS: A front-row seat

Joni Mitchell becomes Companion of Canada

Singer and songwriter Joni Mitchell received Canada's highest award in 2004 when she was made a Companion of the Order of Canada. It was another in a long list of honours for the Saskatchewan-born artist, famous for such songs as "Big Yellow Taxi," "You Turn Me On I'm a Radio," and "Free Man in Paris." Mitchell was already a member of the Canadian Music Hall of Fame, the Cleveland-based Rock and Roll Hall of Fame, and the recipient of a Grammy award for lifetime achievement.

In recent years Mitchell had made it clear that she was fed up with the music business and preferred to spend her time painting. But in 2005 she came out of her painter's studio in Los Angeles long enough to pick 13 of her songs for a CD tribute to Saskatchewan to mark the province's centennial. *Songs of a Prairie Girl* includes the songs "Let the Wind Carry Me," "River" and "Raised on Robbery."

"You carry your childhood with you. Saskatchewan is in my veins," she said.

Gov. Gen. Adrienne Clarkson congratulates Joni Mitchell after presenting her with the Order of Canada in Ottawa in October 2004. (Jonathan Hayward/CP)

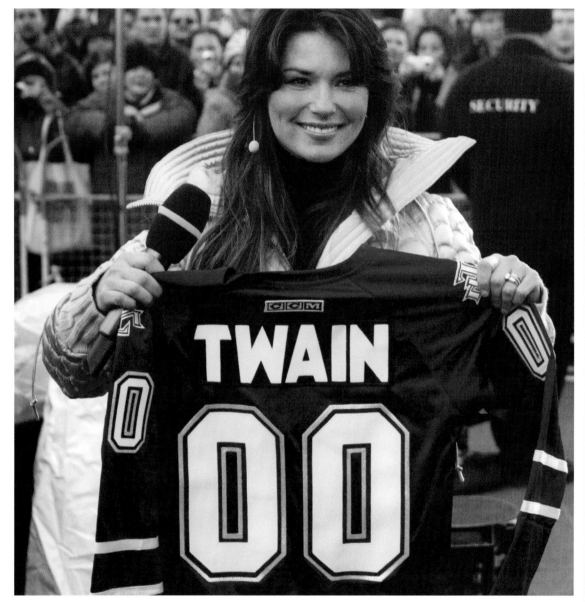

Pierre Berton

Berton cast a towering media shadow across Canada as newspaper columnist, *Maclean's* magazine editor and broadcast personality. But he was best-known for bringing Canada's past to life in dozens of books such as *Klondike: The Last Great Gold Rush*. In his heyday, he sometimes churned out 15,000 words a day. The hallmark of the Berton image was his enthusiasm and immense energy. He loved flamboyant style with his thick white sideburns, huge butterfly-like bow ties and dramatic opera cloaks. He also wrote children's books; of all his books his favourite was *The Secret World of Og*, about his own large brood. Of all his honours and accolades, Berton particularly cherished a letter from a young *Og* fan: "I'm six years old, and this is the best book I ever read in my whole life."

Singer Shania Twain shows off a Maple Leafs jersey presented to her by former Leaf Doug Gilmour in Toronto in November 2004. (Adrian Wyld/CP)

Director David Goyer (bottom) and Canadian actor Ryan Reynolds visit Toronto in November 2004 to promote their new movie, *Blade: Trinity*. (Frank Gunn/CP)

Singer-songwriters Tom Cochrane, Jully Black and Jim Cuddy pose on Parliament Hill in November 2004 after speaking on issues which threatened the Canadian music industry. (Tom Hanson/CP)

Avril Lavigne performs at a concert for tsunami victims in Vancouver in January. (Richard Lam/CP)

1932 - 2005

John Vernon

Vernon was the smarmy Dean Wormer in the sophomoric cult movie *Animal House*. He was a bad guy who got tossed out a window to his death by the even badder Lee Marvin in *Point Blank*. But Canadians may best remember actor John Vernon as a crusading coroner in the groundbreaking 1960s CBC crime series *Wojeck*.

Ryan Larkin, right, watches the 2005 Academy Awards on TV with friends in a Montreal bar. Larkin, who lives on the streets, was the subject of a National Film Board animated short movie that won an Oscar. (Paul Chiasson/CP)

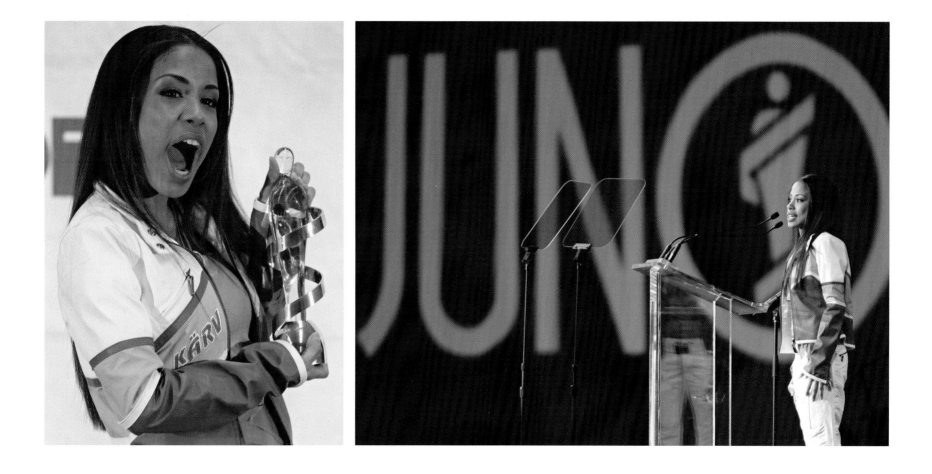

Keisha Chanté accepts the award for best R&B/soul recording at the Junos in Winnipeg in April 2005. (Adrian Wyld/CP)

Actor Kiefer Sutherland, star of the TV series *24*, poses between two RCMP officers at a Canadian Walk of Fame ceremony in Toronto in June 2005. (Tobin Grimshaw/CP)

Domenic Troiano

Troiano, who once played lead guitar for The Guess Who, catapulted to the top of the Canadian music world in the 1960s. He also worked with Ronnie Hawkins, The Mandala, Bush and The James Gang. "His absolute skill as a musician, certainly in the '60s, it was unsurpassed," said Larry LeBlanc, Canadian bureau chief of *Billboard* magazine and Troiano's close friend of 40 years. "Everybody wanted to be Troiano."

Singer/songwriter Paul Anka jokes with the media after being invested into the Order of Canada at Rideau Hall in Ottawa in June 2005. (Tom Hanson/CP)

Dave Grohl of the Foo Fighters performs at The Edge radio station in Toronto in June 2005. (Tobin Grimshaw/CP)

Jim Cuddy of Blue Rodeo plays during the Canadian Live 8 concert in Barrie, Ont., in July. Musicians organized concerts in several cities around the world to pressure Group of Eight countries to give more aid to Africa. (Adrian Wyld/CP)

James Doohan

Best known as the burly chief engineer Scotty on the Starship Enterprise in the original *Star Trek* TV series and films, Doohan also served with the Royal Canadian Artillery and took part in the Juno Beach invasion into France on D-Day.

Gord Downie of the Tragically Hip (left) and Neil Young perform during the finale of the Canadian Live 8 concert. (Aaron Harris/CP)

A fan is tossed in the air during the Jet's performance at the Canadian Live 8 concert. (Adrian Wyld/CP)

Thousands take in the sold-out concert in Barrie. (Nathan Denette/CP)

Oscar marks his 80th with a stamp

Canadian jazz legend Oscar Peterson wipes his eyes in August 2005 after Canada Post introduces a stamp with his picture on it. It was his 80th birthday. (Nathan Denette/CP)

Diana Krall performs at the ceremony, held in Toronto in August 2005. (Nathan Denette/CP)

1938 - 2005

Peter Jennings

The urbane Ottawa-born broadcaster, the face of ABC News, delivered the nightly news to Americans and lots of Canadians over five decades. Along with Tom Brokaw and Dan Rather, he was part of a triumvirate that dominated network news for more than 20 years. The high-school dropout got his broadcasting start on a radio morning show in Ottawa at the age of nine.

New Brunswick firefighter Shelley Ryan shows off her pregnant stomach painted with a Rolling Stones logo as she arrives for their concert in Moncton in September 2005. (Paul Chiasson/CP)

A stagehand is silhouetted against the massive seven-storey stage being built for a Rolling Stones concert at Landsdowne Park in Ottawa in August 2005. (Jonathan Hayward/CP)

Mick Jagger performs during the concert in Ottawa. (Patrick Doyle/CP)

A giant image of Jagger looms on a screen over the stage at Magnetic Hill in Moncton. (Paul Chiasson/CP)

Fans cheer following the first song at the Moncton concert. It was the first time the Stones had performed in Atlantic Canada. They attracted a crowd of almost 85,000, making it the biggest concert in the region's history. (Paul Chiasson/CP)

Isabelle Brasseur and Lloyd Eisler finish their last performance together in Montreal on Oct. 17, 2004. The 1993 world champion pairs skaters were together for 17 years. (Francois Roy/CP)

FROM PUCKS TO BUCKS:
The year in sports

Jockey Lanfranco Dettori does a flying dismount after winning the Canadian International aboard Sulamanni of Ireland at Woodbine Racetrack in Toronto in October 2004. (Frank Gunn/CP)

Jockey Pat Valenzuela celebrates after crossing the finish line on Wild Desert to win the 146th running of the Queen's Plate in Toronto in June 2005. (Adrian Wyld/CP)

Jordan Donich performs his karate routine during sunrise on the Lake Ontario beach in Toronto in November 2004. (Frank Gunn/CP)

Fritz Strobl of Austria collides with a gate as he tumbles through the air during a crash in a training run for a World Cup downhill ski race in Lake Louise, Alta., in November 2004. (Frank Gunn/CP)

Argonauts win Grey Cup

Toronto Argonauts head coach Mike (Pinball) Clemons is doused with Gatorade in the final moments of the 2004 CFL Grey Cup final in Ottawa. The Argonauts beat the B.C. Lions 27-19. (Ryan Remiorz/CP)

Clemons hoists the Grey Cup in celebration after his Argos win the CFL championship. (Ryan Remiorz/CP)

Quarterback Damon Allen of the Toronto Argonauts, left, celebrates with teammates. (Ryan Remiorz/CP)

Erik Guay of Canada soars down the course in a training run for a World Cup downhill ski race in Lake Louise, Alta., in November 2004. (Frank Gunn/CP)

Laval University Rouge et Or players pour Gatorade over head coach Glen Constantin to celebrate their back-to-back Vanier Cup national titles after defeating the University of Saskatchewan Huskies' 7-1 in Hamilton in November 2004. (J.P. Moczulski/CP)

Laval University Rouge et Or players carry the Vanier Cup off the field at Ivor Wynne Stadium. (J.P. Moczulski/CP)

A year without NHL hockey

The National Hockey League was the first major professional league in North America to lose a complete season because of labour strife.

There was no Stanley Cup champion for the first time since 1919.

The NHL set a few records in the 2004-05 season. But they weren't the records fans pay to see.

The NHL owners locked out players at the beginning of the season in a contract dispute over how the league could resolve its financial difficulties. The owners wanted a system of salary caps that would put teams on a spending allowance and lighten paycheques. The players were vehemently opposed to this.

The dispute moved any NHL action from the ice into hotel meeting rooms where the sides, led by the NHL's Gary Bettman and Bob Goodenow of the players' association, bickered and argued over numbers, not pucks. Fans finally got sick of the standoff and turned their attention to other hockey leagues, some vowing they would never pick up the NHL habit again.

Bettman officially cancelled the season in February 2005 and everyone went back to their locker rooms to lick their wounds. Talks began again in May and by July the two had an agreement that forced many teams to restructure their squads to adhere to salary caps. Players were not happy but wanted to get back to the game.

"There was no winner, however, in this contest," said hockey legend Wayne Gretzky, a part owner of the Phoenix Coyotes. "At the end of the day everybody lost. We almost crippled our industry."

Wayne Gretzky listens to a question as he speaks with media in Toronto in November 2004.
(Adrian Wyld/CP)

Fans give their view of the NHL lockout at a hockey game in Katowice, Poland, between the Worldstars and the Polish national team in December 2004. (Paul Chiasson/CP)

118

NHL commissioner Gary Bettman answers questions in New York in February after cancelling the 2004-2005 hockey season. (Paul Chiasson/CP)

Bettman shakes hands with Bob Goodenow, executive director of the National Hockey League Players' Association, in Toronto in July 2005 after players vote in favour of a settlement. (Adrian Wyld/CP)

Goodenow speaks at a news conference in Toronto in March 2005. (Aaron Harris/CP)

The Montreal Canadiens dressing room remains empty at the Bell Centre in Montreal in February 2005. (Paul Chiasson/CP)

Hockey Hall of Fame inductees show off their rings at a ceremony in Toronto in November 2004. Left to right: Cliff Fletcher, Larry Murphy, Paul Coffey and Ray Bourque. (Frank Gunn/CP)

Hockey player Steve Moore, seriously injured when he was sucker-punched on the ice by Todd Bertuzzi of the Vancouver Canucks 11 months earlier, makes a statement in Toronto in December 2004 as his brothers Marc and Dominic look on. Moore asked the B.C. attorney general to investigate why Bertuzzi's plea bargain was allowed to proceed without Moore present in the courtroom. (Adrian Wyld/CP)

NHL star Todd Bertuzzi, accompanied by his wife, Julie, arrive at court in Vancouver in December 2004. Bertuzzi pleaded guilty to assault causing bodily harm for sucker-punching Steve Moore of the Colorado Avalanche. (Chuck Stoody/CP)

Canada's juniors win gold

Team Canada celebrates after defeating Russia 6-1 to win the gold medal at the world junior hockey championships in Grand Forks, N.D., in January 2005. (Ryan Remiorz/CP)

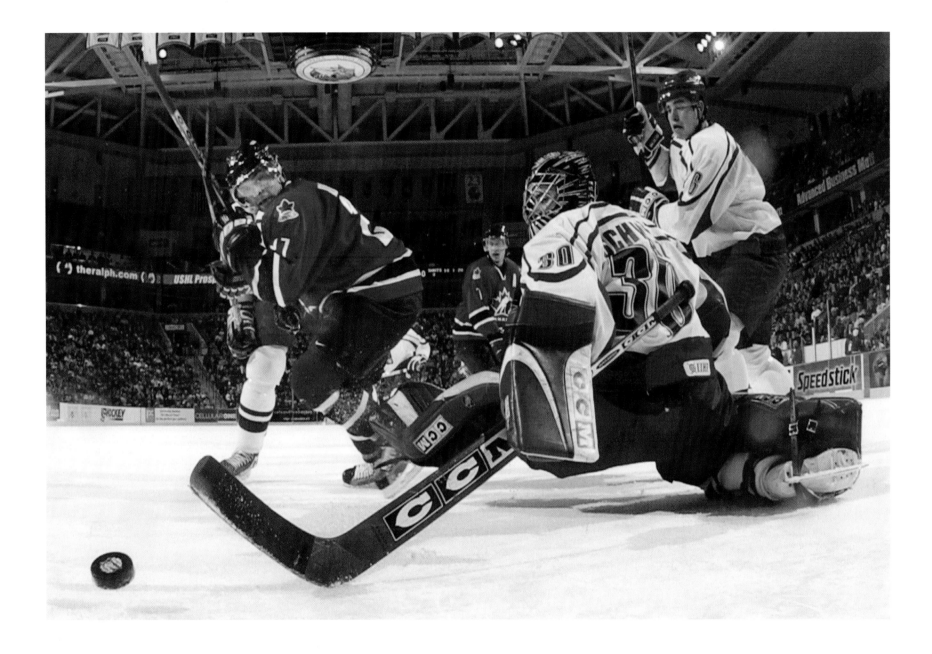

Nigel Dawes, left, of Canada scores on goaltender Marek Schwarz of the Czech Republic in semifinal action. (Dave Sanford/CP/Pool)

Members of Team Canada huddle before their game against Finland. (Jonathan Hayward/CP)

Team Canada's Patrice Bergeron, left, Sidney Crosby, centre, and Corey Perry, right, celebrate after their gold-medal win. (Ryan Remiorz/CP)

Marie-France Dubreuil and Patrice Lauzon of Montreal perform their free dance to win the gold medal in the ice dance competition at the Canadian figure skating championships in 2005 in London, Ont. (Paul Chiasson/CP)

Centre Chris Bosh (4) of the Toronto Raptors collides with guard Kevin Martin (23) and forward Darius Songaila (right) of the Sacramento Kings during an NBA game in Toronto in January 2005. (Frank Gunn/CP)

Jennifer Heil of Montreal practises her jump in the moguls run in January 2005 at a competition in Mont-Tremblant, Que. (Jacques Boissinot/CP)

Jeremy Wotherspoon skates in the men's 500-metre event during World Cup speed skating in Calgary in January 2005. (Jeff McIntosh/CP)

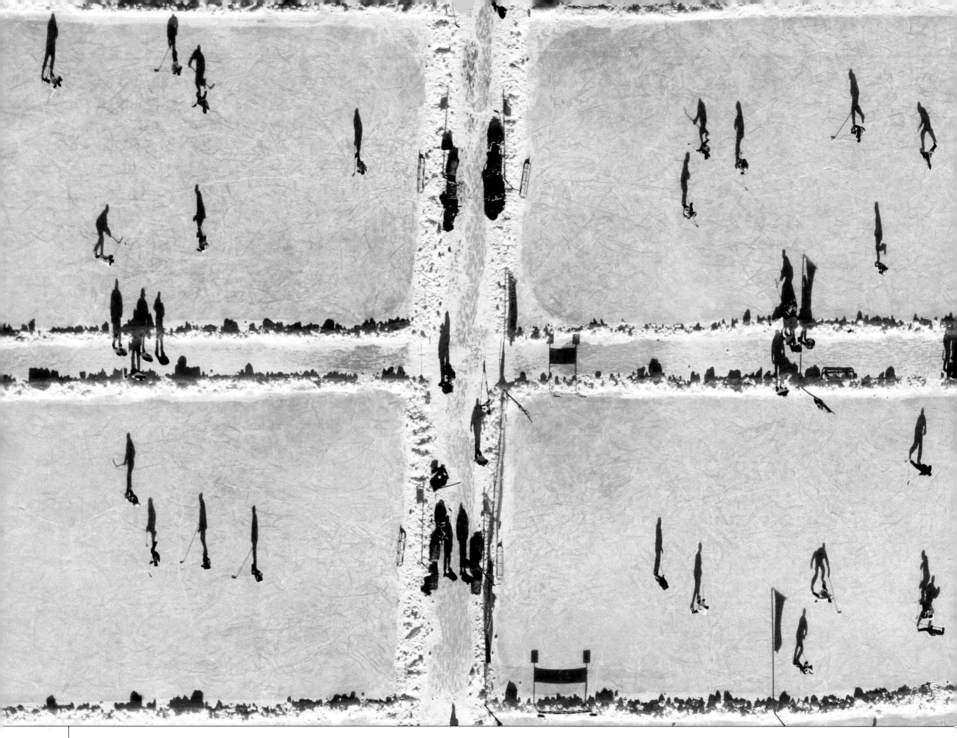

Hockey players cast shadows on Roulston Pond during the world pond hockey tournament in Plaster Rock, N.B., in February 2005. Ninety-six teams competed. (Ryan Remiorz/CP)

Teams compete side by side on Roulston Pond at the world pond hockey tournament. (Ryan Remiorz/CP)

Kerstin Juergens of Germany competes at the world skeleton championships in Calgary in February 2005. (Jeff McIntosh/CP)

Canada's Pierre Lueders, foreground, followed by teammates Ken Kotyk, Morgan Alexander and Lascelles Brown, jump into their sled during the four-man bobsleigh competition. (Jeff McIntosh/CP)

Canada's Jayson Krause, left, and Florian Linder, compete in the two-man bobsleigh contest. (Jeff McIntosh/CP)

New champs reign in curling

Team Canada skip Colleen Jones reacts after being eliminated from play at the Canadian women's curling championships in St. John's, Nfld., in February 2005. (Andrew Vaughan/CP)

Manitoba skip Jennifer Jones is embraced by lead Cathy Gathier after winning the Canadian curling championship. (Andrew Vaughan/CP)

Ontario skip Wayne Middaugh slides through the house as he delivers a shot at the Canadian men's curling championships in Edmonton in March 2005. (Adrian Wyld/CP)

Alberta second Scott Pfeifer hugs skip Randy Ferbey after their win over Nova Scotia at the men's curling championships. (Tom Hanson/CP)

Team Canada skip Jennifer Jones reacts to a bad shot against Sweden at the 2005 world women's curling championship in Paisley, Scotland. Canada lost. (Andrew Vaughan/CP)

Men's silver medallist Jeffrey Buttle of Smooth Rock Falls, Ont., performs his free program at the world figure skating championships in Moscow in March 2005. (Paul Chiasson/CP)

Men's gold medallist Stephane Lambiel (centre) of Switzerland shares the podium with silver medallist Jeffrey Buttle, left, of Canada and bronze medallist Evan Lysacek of the United States at the medal ceremonies. (Paul Chiasson/CP)

Buttle smiles as his marks are posted for his short program at the competition. (Paul Chiasson/CP)

Team Canada players gather in a ritual circle at the end of a pre-game skate in April 2005 at the world women's championship in Linkoping, Sweden. (Jacques Boissinot/CP)

Heart-breaker in Sweden for Canada's women

Team Canada players (from the left) Delaney Collins, Carla MacLeod, and Vicky Sunohara react after their team loses the final to the United States in a shootout. (Jacques Boissinot/CP)

Captain Cassie Campbell of Team Canada absorbs her team's loss to the United States at the world women's hockey championship. Canada won the silver medal. (Jacques Boissinot/CP)

Nicole Godfrey (left) and Kelly McKee cheer for the Canadian women at the championship. (Jacques Boissinot/CP)

Fans fill the Rogers Centre as the Toronto Blue Jays play their home opener against the Boston Red Sox in April 2005. (Frank Gunn/CP)

Centre-fielder Vernon Wells of the Toronto Blue Jays dives unsuccessfully for a long ball off the bat of Chris Gomez of the Baltimore Orioles during a baseball game in Toronto in June 2005. (Frank Gunn/CP)

A fan holds up a sign as Sidney Crosby of the Rimouski Oceanic serves a penalty during the Memorial Cup final in London, Ont., in May 2005. (Adrian Wyld/CP)

Members of the London Knights touch the Memorial Cup trophy that was theirs after they defeated the Rimouski Oceanic. (Nathan Denette/CP)

Team USA forward Eric Cole (left) gets mauled by Team Canada defenceman Robyn Regehr at the world hockey championship in Innsbruck, Austria, in May 2005. (Frank Gunn/CP)

Team Canada's Simon Gagne (21), Ed Jovanovski (55), Dan Boyle (27), Joe Thornton (97) and Rick Nash (top right of group) celebrate a goal by Thornton. Team USA goaltender Rick DiPietro (top) watches. (Frank Gunn/CP)

Canada's Paul Tracy races to the provisional pole position during qualification at a Champ Car race in Toronto in July 2005. (Tobin Grimshaw/CP)

Sauber's Jacques Villeneuve rounds the track to place ninth at the Canadian Grand Prix in Montreal in June 2005. (Paul Chiasson/CP)

World aquatics championships come to Montreal

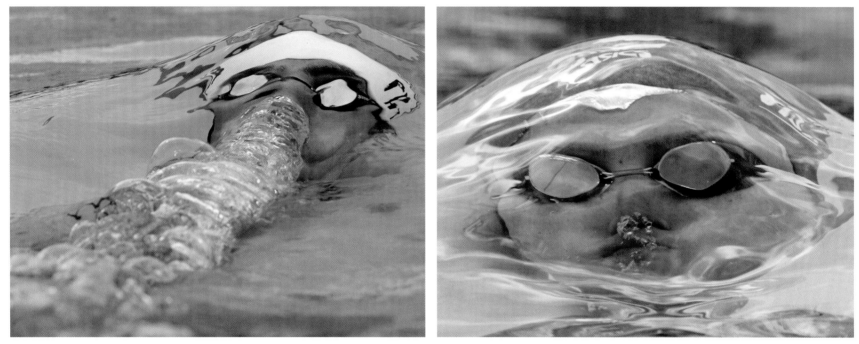

Michael Phelps of the United States (left) and Reiko Nakamura of Japan (right) leave a trail of bubbles as they surface while swimming their heats at the world aquatics championships in Montreal in July 2005. (Frank Gun/CP)

Chelsea Davis of the United States hits the board in the preliminary round of the women's three-metre springboard diving competition at the aquatics championships. (Ryan Remiorz/CP)

Jia Hu of China shows the form that won him the gold medal in of the men's 10-metre diving competition. (Frank Gunn/CP)

Alexandre Despatie of Canada poses with his two gold medals for the one- and three-metre springboard competitions. (Ryan Remiorz/CP)

Emilie Heymans of Canada shows her unhappiness with one of her dives in the women's 10-metre platform final. She placed fourth. (Frank Gunn/CP)

Alexandre Despatie performs in the final round of the men's one-metre springboard. (Tom Hanson/CP)

Canada's men's 2x200-metre freestyle team displays their silver medals. From the left: Andrew Hurd, Rick Say, Colin Russell and Brent Hayden. (Frank Gunn/CP)

Team Canada performs in the synchronized swimming event. (Tom Hanson/CP)

Steve Nash of the Phoenix Suns holds his NBA Most Valuable Player trophy at a game in May 2005. Nash was the first Canadian to win the award. (Kevork Djansezian/AP)

Nash high-fives a young basketball player at his charity basketball game in Toronto in July. (Adrian Wyld/CP)

Charlie Bell, right, of the U.S. team, tries to steal the ball from Denham Brown of Canada during a qualifying tournament in the Dominican Republic for the 2006 world basketball championships. (Andres Leighton/AP)

Perdita Felicien, of Pickering, Ont., leaps over the final hurdle on her way to winning the women's 100-metre hurdles at the national senior outdoor championships in Winnipeg in July. (Marianne Helm/CP)

Jack Nicklaus walks onto the 18th green during the final day of the Telus Skins Game in Whistler, B.C., in July 2005. Canadian Stephen Ames won with seven skins and $150,000; Nicklaus was second with seven skins and $120,000. (Chuck Stoody/CP)

Left: First-round pick Sidney Crosby of Dartmouth, N.S., holds up his new Pittsburgh Penguins jersey with team owner Mario Lemieux (right) at the NHL draft in July 2005. Right: Crosby holds his first news conference as a Penguin. (Tobin Grimshaw/CP)

Regina welcomes the Canada Games

Athletes from across Canada gather in a circle to form an aboriginal medicine wheel during the closing ceremonies at the Canada Summer Games in Regina in August 2005. (Fred Chartrand/CP)

Ryan Bradley of British Columbia is tackled by Matt O'Leary of Ontario during the men's gold-medal rugby final at the Games. British Columbia won the gold medal and Ontario the bronze. (Jacques Boissinot/CP)

Emma Brightwell of Ontario grimaces as she is pinned down by Leah Callahan of British Columbia during women's team wrestling. (Fred Chartrand/CP)

Top left: Kayaker Hannah Vaughan of Nova Scotia displays two gold medals she won in the K-1 1,000-metre and K-2 1,000-metre. Bottom left: Vaughan celebrates her win. Right: Maryse Thivierge and Catherine Lariviere-Gauthier of Quebec race in the women's C-2 1,000-metre final to a gold medal finish. (Jacques Boissinot/CP)

The main pack pedals on the highway during the men's road race in Lumsden, Sask. (Jacques Boissinot/CP)

Kim Clijsters of Belgium kicks her way through 20 centimetres of water that gathered on centre court during a rain delay in the quarter-finals at the Rogers Cup in Toronto in August 2005. (Frank Gunn/CP)

Rafael Nadal of Spain celebrates after beating Andre Agassi of the United States to win the final at the Rogers Cup tennis tournament in Montreal in August 2005. (Paul Chiasson/CP)

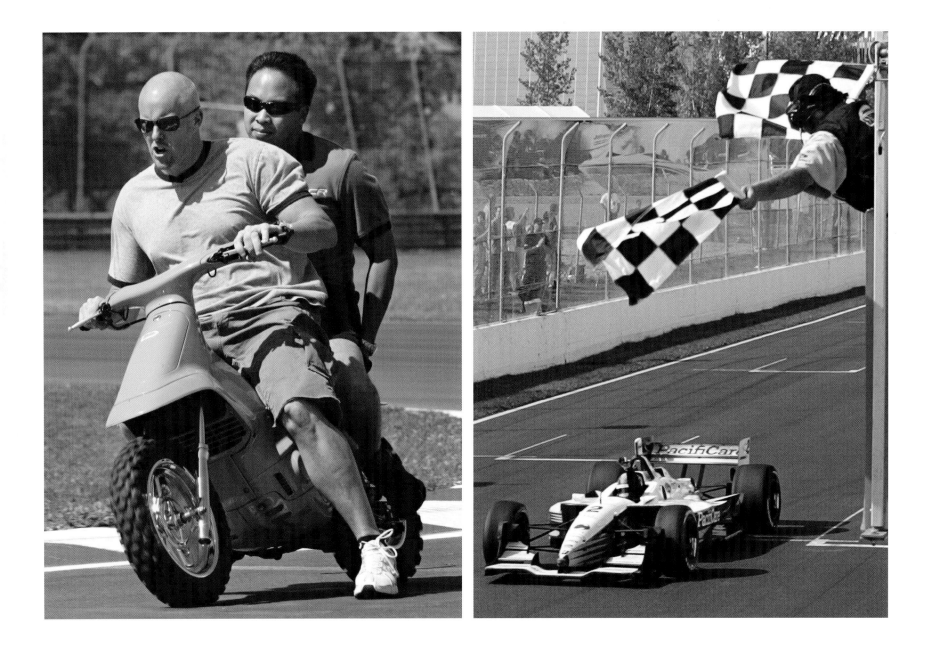

Champ Car driver Paul Tracy, left, drives his scooter around the circuit Gilles Villeneuve in Montreal before the Molson Indy in August 2005. (Ryan Remiorz/CP)

Spain's Oriol Servia takes the checkered flag to win the Indy's Champ Car race. (Ryan Remiorz/CP)

Davin Bush and T.J. Stancil of the Saskatchewan Roughriders tackle Paris Jackson of the B.C. Lions (top) at a CFL game in Regina in August 2005. (Troy Fleece/CP)

John Hewitt hams it up for photographers before the so-called Hockey Enforcers Black and Blue event in Prince George, B.C., in August. About 2,000 people watched hockey players duke it out with each other for 60 seconds or until the referee called a halt. (Richard Lam/CP)

Former NHL enforcer Kent Carlson throws a punch at Mark Raiter during the first round of the Hockey Enforcers fight. (Richard Lam/CP)

PASSAGES: People we will remember

Notables

John Baldry, 64

A British blues legend nicknamed Long John because of his six-foot-seven-inch height, he helped launch the careers of rock greats like Rod Stewart and the Rolling Stones. "He gave me a start in his band and had a knack for discovering and mentoring talent … I will miss him," said Stewart. Baldry, who became a Canadian citizen in 1981, released more than 40 albums of his own.

Marc Baltzan, 75

An outspoken supporter of medicare, Baltzan was a pioneer of kidney transplantation. In 1963, he was on the medical team that performed the second kidney transplant in Canada. He was also instrumental in introducing new kidney treatments to Saskatchewan, his home province.

Wilfred Bigelow, 91

Described as the father of open-heart surgery in Canada, Bigelow invented the technique of hypothermia – deliberately cooling the heart to make surgery safer – and performed the world's first such procedure on a dog in 1949.

Edward Bronfman, 77

Along with his brother Peter, Bronfman developed a business empire that branched into much of the Canadian economy. The holdings of the so-called Edper-Bronfman group ranged from Royal Trust, London Life and real estate broker Royal Le Page to property developer Bramalea, forest company MacMillan Bloedel, brewer Labatt and the Montreal Canadiens hockey club.

Earl Cameron, 89

Once described as Canadian as wheat, Cameron began his career at CBC as a radio announcer. He won the job reading the 11 p.m. TV news in 1959 and for the next seven years he was the face of TV news in Canada. "If Earl said it, you knew it was true and that even with all the miseries, all was well with the world," said Knowlton Nash, one of his successors as anchor.

Harold Cardinal, 60

A respected aboriginal leader, teacher and author, Cardinal became the youngest person to be elected president of the Indian Association of Alberta.

Terry Carisse, 62

A country music singer-songwriter known for penning songs including "Sparkle in her Eyes" and "Love Sweet Love", Carisse released seven albums in the 1970s and '80s and had 32 charted singles in Canada.

Henry Corden, 85

Born in Montreal, Corden went on to fame in the cartoon world as the voice of caveman Fred Flintstone. He took over the famous "yabba dabba doo" in 1977, when the original voice, Allen Reed, died. Corden tweaked his role to approximate Jackie Gleason's character Ralph Kramden, from TV's *The Honeymooners*.

Independent MP Chuck Cadman stands outside his apartment building in Ottawa in May 2005. (Tom Hanson/CP)

James Houston, 83

A guiding spirit behind Inuit carving and printmaking, Houston encouraged Inuit to produce more of the carvings they had first begun to make in the 19th century to trade with Arctic whalers. The market he helped create put food on many Arctic tables.

Bob Hunter, 63

A reporter and co-founder of the environmental group Greenpeace, Hunter helped bring public attention to such issues as nuclear testing and the excesses of whaling and seal hunting. *Time* magazine once named him one of the top eco-heroes of the 20th century.

Heath Lamberts, 63

Described as "naturally funny," the actor performed at the Stratford and Shaw festivals and was especially known for his performance in the title role of Cyrano de Bergerac. He was also part of the original cast of *Beauty and the Beast*.

Charlotte MacLeod, 82

Born in New Brunswick, MacLeod moved to the United States as a young child. She wrote more than 30 "cozy" mysteries in the style of Agatha Christie that sold more than one million copies. Under such titles as *The Convivial Codfish* and *Exit the Milkman*, her books often featured amateur sleuths. She also published books under the pen name Alisa Craig that were set in Canada.

Bob McAdorey, 69

With his trademark curly hair and Buddy Holly-type horned rim glasses, McAdorey helped set the musical agenda for a generation of teens as a DJ at CHUM radio in Toronto. In the 1960s, CHUM was the station to listen to and McAdorey was the man who decided if a song was going places. He later became an entertainment personality on Global Television.

Christina McCall, 70

A political writer, McCall helped coin the phrase "he haunts us still" about former prime minister Pierre Trudeau. McCall combined a journalism career with literary non-fiction writing and with her husband, Stephen Clarkson, published two volumes on Trudeau. "She was the premier political analyst of her generation," said Clarkson.

John Morgan, 74

One of the original cast members of the long-running CBC comedy, *Royal Canadian Air Farce*, Morgan's roles included the dim-witted Mike from Canmore. When asked once about the success of the show, Morgan said: "You know what they say: we use satire against our leaders; Americans shoot theirs."

Tom Patterson, 84

Patterson is credited with founding the Stratford Festival in 1953. The Second World War veteran and former magazine editor managed to attract well-known Shakespearean director Tyrone Guthrie to a tiny farming community in southwestern Ontario to run the festival, first held in a tent. Guthrie, in turn, attracted stars like Alec Guinness, earning the theatre company an international reputation.

Louis Robichaud, 79

For 10 years beginning in 1960 Robichaud was the first Acadian premier of New Brunswick and is credited with modernizing the province. The small-town lawyer introduced the province's Official Languages Act.

Alex Shibicky, 91

The first hockey player to use a slapshot, Shibicky was a member of the New York Rangers' 1940 Stanley Cup team. Shibicky said he learned it in practice from teammate Fred (Bun) Cook during the 1935-36 season and applied it in a game in 1937. "It was a snap shot from the hip," said his son, Alex.

Robin Spry, 65

A filmmaker best known for his documentary on the October Crisis, Spry had a long career as a documentary maker, director, writer and producer in film and television.

Louis Sutter, 73

He raised seven sons, and six of them played in the NHL. A legend in Viking, Alta., Sutter "took great pride in all of his boys," said Viking Mayor Garry Wolosinka. Sons Darryl, Brian, Duane, Brent, Rich and Ron all played NHL hockey for five seasons in the 1980s and continued to be involved in hockey after their careers on the ice ended.

Lewis Urry, 77

As a chemical engineer at National Carbon Co., Urry invented the long-lasting batteries that power portable devices such as Walkmans. While working on ways to improve the short-lived carbon zinc batteries, he came up with a practical alkaline battery that used powdered zinc as the electrolyte.

Scott Young, 87

A journalist, author and the father of pop star Neil Young, Young covered the Second World War, the assassination of John F. Kennedy and nearly every major sporting event in North America. He worked for a variety of media outlets, including the *Winnipeg Free Press*, The Canadian Press, *The Globe and Mail*, *Maclean's* magazine and the *Toronto Telegram*.

1967: Robert Stanfield is congratulated by John Diefenbaker after he wins the job of replacing him as leader of the federal Progressive Conservatives. (Peter Hall/CP)

STIRRING UP THE PAST:
Images of yesterday

1974: Conservative Leader Robert Stanfield drops a football while campaigning in North Bay, Ont. (Doug Ball/CP)

1977: Pierre Trudeau pirouettes after others, including the Queen, leave a formal photo session at Buckingham Palace in London. (Doug Ball/CP)

1976: Agriculture Minister Eugene Whelan is hit on the head with a milk jug during an Ottawa demonstration by dairy farmers angry about an enforced drop in milk production levels. (Russell Mant/CP)

1976: René Lévesque, just elected Quebec's first separatist premier, speaks to Parti Québécois party supporters and reporters on election night. (CP Photo)

1990: Soldier Patrick Cloutier and Saskatchewan aboriginal Brad Laroque come face to face in a tense standoff at the Kahnesatake reserve in Oka, Que. (Shaney Komulainen/CP)

1954: Igor Gouzenko, whose revelations led to the cracking of a Soviet spy ring in Canada in 1946, is shown with a copy of his book, *The Fall of a Titan*. (CP Photo)

2001: Protesters hurl part of a fence and a traffic pylon at riot police during protests at the Summit of the Americas in Quebec City. (Paul Chiasson/CP)

1975: Magician Allen Allen, suspended over the Rideau Canal in Ottawa, attempts to free himself from chains before a burning rope gives way. He managed to escape. (Fred Chartrand/CP)

1970: A newsboy holds up a newspaper reporting the invoking of the War Measures Act, the first time it had been used in peacetime. The move came after the kidnapping of British diplomat James Cross and Quebec Labour Minister Pierre Laporte by the terrorist FLQ. (Peter Bregg/CP)

2002: Canadian troops launch their assault on the Whale's Back in eastern Afghanistan. The troops joined American soldiers for combat operations as part of the war on terrorism. (Stephen Thorne/CP)

1985: Betty Walsh peers through a broken window into a neighbour's cabin, one of several overturned by tornadoes that ripped through the area around Barrie, Ont., killing a dozen people and leaving hundreds homeless. (Tim Clark/CP)

1978: Queen Elizabeth waves to children from the back of a train as she departs Fort Qu'Appelle, Sask. (Doug Ball/CP)

1989: Elizabeth, the Queen Mother, inspects a Guard of Honour on Parliament Hill. (Ron Poling/CP)

1984: Pierre Trudeau leaves 24 Sussex Drive in his 1959 Mercedes sports car after resigning as prime minister. (Andrew Vaughan/CP)

2005: Justin Trudeau, Pierre Trudeau's eldest son, leaves the church with his new bride Sophie Gregoire in his father's Mercedes after their wedding in Montreal. (Ryan Remiorz/CP)

1995: A huge Canadian flag is passed along a crowd in Montreal to support Canadian unity on the eve of the Quebec referendum on sovereignty. (Ryan Remiorz/CP)

1998: Celine Dion blows a kiss to hockey star Maurice (The Rocket) Richard, who was in the audience at the Montreal concert. (Robert Galbraith/CP)

1984: A child reaches out to touch Pope John Paul II as he walks through a crowd at Montreal's Notre Dame Cathedral. (Fred Chartrand/CP)

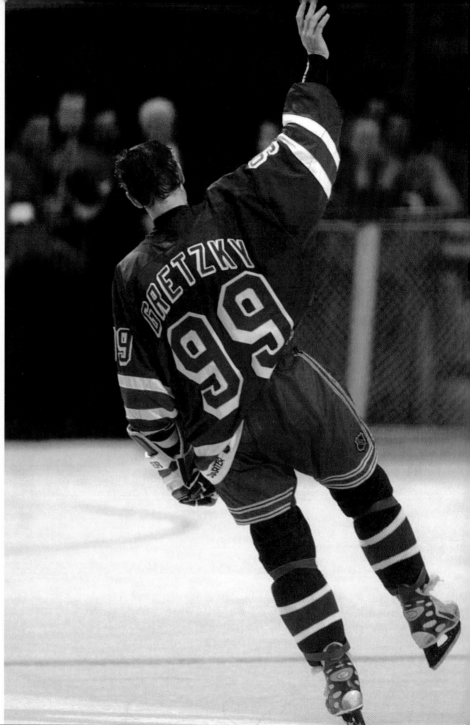

1997: Ballerina Karen Kain takes off her shoes on stage in Winnipeg, while performing in her last role for the National Ballet of Canada. (Fred Greenslade/CP)

1999: Hockey great Wayne Gretzky waves as he makes his exit from the rink at the Corel Centre in Kanata, Ont., after playing his last NHL game in Canada. He announced his retirement the next day. (Fred Chartrand/CP)